MW00411775

My Lemonade Recipe:

Turning Life's Sour Experiences Into Something Sweet

―――

CHANTÉ DENT

Contents

Acknowledgements I
About the Author II
From My Heart to Yours III

PART I - THE LEMONS

From Broken to Beautiful 1
My Pain 2
The Turning Point 7
She Changed Me 9

PART II - THE INGREDIENTS

You Alone 15
My Process 16
Fighting for Emotional Freedom 17
Damaged or Defined? 21
Forgiveness, Love, and Mercy 23

PART III - THE LEMONADE

Heal. Love. Live. 31
My Purpose 32
What Matters Most 34
Joy 36
Your Turn 37

ACKNOWLEDGEMENTS

My Heavenly Father:

Father God, if You had not sent Your son Jesus Christ to die on the cross for my sins so that I could be redeemed and set free, none of me, none of this would exist. Glory to Your name! Thank You Jesus for Your unconditional love.

My husband:

Howard, I love you! Thank you for always encouraging me and cheering me on. Your support, your love, and patience mean more to me than you may ever know. I am so grateful to stand with you as we parent our children and serve the Lord together.

My family:

Thank you Lord for my Bandy / Garrison roots. They run strong and deep. The love we bare for one another helped me through the storm. Thank you family for being my example of what love and strength look like.

BAWAR (Bay Area Women Against Rape):

You trained me, encouraged me, and gave me the first opportunity to help survivors heal, love, and live again. Thank you.

Friends and Supporters:

You all are more than amazing! You have seen the ups and the downs and I appreciate each of you. Thank you for your prayers and support.

About the Author

Chanté Dent is the founder and director of Earnest Love, Inc. She received her Bachelor of Science degree in Sociology from California State University, East Bay and currently volunteers as a member of the RAINN (Rape, Abuse & Incest National Network) Speakers Bureau.

As a young girl Chanté was sexually abused by two of her cousins, and during adulthood, she experienced acquaintance rape. It became her norm to sweep those traumatic events under the rug. During the beginning stages of her healing process from rape, she realized she had been wearing a mask and not truly dealing with the painful aftermath of sexual trauma. She quickly learned that if she wanted to enjoy her life and live in freedom, her wounded emotions would have to heal. Her healing journey was not easy, but it was well worth it. Today, Chanté is a devoted teacher, speaker, and author, who helps victims of sexual trauma transition from survivors to overcomers so that they thrive in life.

Chanté enjoys all things outdoors; nature is her peaceful place. She resides in Suwanee, GA with her husband and their two children. One of her favorite scriptures is 2 Corinthians 5:17 – *"Therefore, if anyone is in Christ, the new creation has come: The old has gone, the new is here!"*. She firmly believes that God can take your shattered pieces and create a beautiful masterpiece if you let Him.

From My Heart to Yours

I initially felt that my experiences were to be tucked away and never shared. But the moment I realized my transparency could help someone, I made the decision to write my story. My desire was to be a source of hope to those who feel hopeless. I wanted to encourage and inspire anyone who wonders if there really is a light at the end of the tunnel. God turned my situation around, and I believe He can do the same for you.

As you read, I pray God will use the words of this book to strengthen you. He loves you so much! Your connecting with me through this book is just one way for Him to remind you that you are not alone. If you fear people will judge you and choose not to understand your experience; you are not alone. If shame, guilt, confusion, fear, or embarrassment keeps you silent; you are not alone. If you are tired of hurting, tired of being depressed, and ready to be free then you are not alone. Our journeys might not be the same, but our desired destination is. We desire to be free from a past that is painful: to move forward with an undeniable confidence that life is worth living and we will live it to the fullest.

Some may say, "Why are you sharing your story?" Well, I believe it is important that we talk about the great things God has done for us. Our testimony also encourages others and reminds them that healing and restoration can be theirs too! It has not always been easy sharing my story. At one point, I was embarrassed and engulfed with secrecy. I confided with only a few people during that time and mostly used journaling to process my thoughts. Throughout this book, I will not only tell you my story, but I will also share a few excerpts from my journal as well.

"When life gives you lemons, make lemonade!" is a proverbial phrase used to lift your spirit and give hope when experiencing the trials of life. After hearing my testimony, someone referred to it as the "Lemonade Recipe". I was given a bag of lemons. They were extremely sour and they were not going anywhere. What was I to do with these sour lemons? I had a lot of other ingredients; some were pleasant and some were not pleasant. I longed for God to give me the best lemonade recipe possible with the ingredients I had, and that He did! He added His thoughts and ideas. God's heart united with my own developed this sweet and refreshing recipe. Now I would like to share a fresh glass with you in my book, *My Lemonade Recipe*: *Turning Life's Sour Experiences Into Something Sweet*.

PART I

The Lemons

FROM BROKEN TO BEAUTIFUL

Lord, I need You to hold me
In a way that I have never been held before
These tears are painful
Fragile emotions
Empty heart
I need to be restored

I am so broken
Hurt and confused
And I wonder
This life, can You still use?

Guide me in darkness
Lord, please give me strength
Make me whole
From broken to beautiful
Beauty for ashes

My Pain

As a young girl, my older cousins took advantage of me and abused their authority. I was touched inappropriately and told to perform inappropriate sexual acts. Afterwards, I was told that if I said anything I would get in trouble. So, I did not tell anyone. At age 25, I was raped, and again, I did not tell. With each violation, I experienced shock and silently battled shame, guilt, regret, hate, and anger.

I had a history with the man who raped me. I had been sexually active with him in the past. I knew it had to end and it did. Being violated by him months later was the last thing I saw coming. He was a massage therapist and I had an appointment at his in-home office. Knowing these particular details about the man who violated me lead some people to believe that I asked for it, or that I should have known. The truth is I did not know and I definitely did not ask for it.

What began professional quickly became very uncomfortable. This was someone I knew and trusted. I remember trying to push him off, asking him what he was doing, and telling him to stop! When he finally stopped I did not run away hysterically; I went into the restroom and tried to get myself together. When I returned to the massage room, he tried to comfort me by asking if I wanted to continue with the massage. I was sickened by this question.

It was strange. He raped me, and then he tried to comfort me. I was in dire need of someone to comfort me. He was the only one around and I did not want to believe what had just happened. Oddly, he attempted to have intercourse. In an effort to erase the pain, I allowed him to. I tried to fix it. I wanted to categorize what had taken place moments earlier as sex. I did not want to remember the shock of him turning on me and forcing himself on me. I remember thinking that if I could just let him do this, I would not remember that he just violated me. I laid there numb with my head turned to the side, crying inwardly. As I lay there, I hoped and really believed that once I got up everything would be okay. When he finished, he left the room. I recall shaking and being in a daze. My defense mechanism was supposed to make the pain go away, but it did not. I was violated and the pain and the memory remained.

As I walked out of the room, I saw his sister sitting on the couch. I walked past her, staring and could not speak. I wondered if she heard me as I resisted her brother. Was she there? Did she hear me telling him to stop? He walked me to my car and neither of us spoke a word. It was an eerie silence. I drove away and began crying uncontrollably. As soon as I entered my home, I immediately took a shower. I was overwhelmed with tears and pain, as I tried to wash it all way.

A month later still silent and dead inside, I was trying my best to cope and internalize the aftermath of rape. One day while taking a coffee break at work, tears began to flow. I was a mess and wanted to quit my job and give up on life. Thankfully, I had a supervisor who would not let me do that. A few days later, I felt ill and left work early. When I arrived home, I told my mom I was sick. She suggested that I call the advice nurse. After I told the nurse my symptoms, she responded, "You either have the stomach flu, or you're pregnant. When was the last time you had sex?" At that moment, I was taken back to the day I was raped. How was I supposed to process this and relive what happened? The thought of having to dig up what I chose to bury and never share was overwhelming. In a trance, I softly murmured, "But I told him no." I could faintly hear the nurse saying, "Ma'am, ma'am, what did you say? Ma'am, are you there?" When I was able to speak, I briefly explained what happened about a month ago. As a mandated reporter, the nurse immediately had a police officer on the phone with us.

She also dispatched a police officer and an ambulance to my home. At that point my family became aware that I had been raped. What an overwhelming experience. The EMTs patiently waited outside of my home to take me to the hospital. I did not feel comfortable riding in an ambulance, so the police gave me the option of my dad taking me to the hospital. In preparation to write the report, the police officer asked if I was comfortable with my parents being present. Although I was not, I agreed to let my parents stay in the room. I did not want them to feel like I was trying to hide anything from them. I soon realized giving the report in their presence was not the best decision. It was very uncomfortable giving the details of the violation. I omitted some details that day; it was just too hard to share in front of my parents.

Since I no longer had the address of where the assault had taken place, the police officer needed me to point out the location. After the written report was complete, my father and I entered the patrol car. As we approached the house the officer instructed me to duck so I would not chance being identified. Once we returned to our house, my family and I went to the hospital and the doctor confirmed that I was pregnant. Everything I tried to bury had resurfaced in the most inconvenient way. That night on the hospital bed, I broke down. As far as I was concerned, my life was over. My mom tried to comfort me, but I began yelling, "Don't touch me! Where is my dad?" I was hysterical. During that whole time, the Word of God flowed from the mouths of my parents. They were not going to let their daughter fight this fight alone. Later that night, my nephew who was only four years old at the time, joined in to comfort me by saying, "It's okay Auntie, everything is going to be okay". He did not know the details, he only knew Auntie was awfully hurt. Those simple words melted my heart and gave me hope.

Initially I did not want to press charges. Filing the police report was distressing and I did not know if I could handle much more. I was then informed that there was a young lady who had a similar experience with the same man. She was willing to talk to the police with me if I needed her to. Hearing this angered me even more. I called the detective assigned to my case to let her know that I wanted to press charges. I shared my story again, including the details I did not feel comfortable sharing in the presence of my parents during the initial report. The detective suggested I come to the police station and place a recorded phone call to the man who raped me. She explained that I would ask my offender a series of police appointed questions that would allow him to incriminate himself with his answers. I followed through with her suggestion. A dear friend accompanied me to the police station where I nervously placed the phone call. He admitted to what he did. He also apologized. He said he did not know what came over him and did not mean to hurt me.

Months later I received a call from the detective informing me that the District Attorney would not be able move forward with my case. She explained the reasoning why: 1) I reported the assault and had changed my mind about pressing charges 2) I gave additional details to the detective, including that I had been sexually active months before the assault, which I had not included in the initial report. She further explained that although my story and his coincided it would be difficult to prove beyond reasonable doubt. She also mentioned that it would be difficult to prove if the child was conceived during the violation or afterwards when I "consented". Pregnant or not, meant to hurt me or not, I was raped and that was my reality. The District Attorney chose not to move forward with my case, but I had to move forward with my life.

My Journal Entry
#1

I know exactly what happened to me on that gloomy day. I know exactly what it felt like to be forced to do something I had absolutely no interest in doing. I know exactly how it felt to participate in order to survive mentally and emotionally....and in the end, that's all that matters. Though devastated at the outcome, I do feel some vindication because he acknowledged TO ME what he had done.

      Soon after, I had my first appointment with an obstetrician. It was extremely uncomfortable. To add to my discomfort she was a doctor whom I had never seen before. I cried the entire time. Thankfully, the doctor was very sensitive to my needs. She was a woman of God who provided the utmost support throughout my pregnancy. After that appointment, she referred me to a psychologist. I scheduled a visit. While sitting in the waiting room, I reached a high level of anger and told my sister to take me home. I did not want to sit and talk about what happened again. My mom, in her wisdom, had a brief heart to heart with me. She encouraged me to talk. She told me that if I did not deal with it, I would not heal from it. I am so thankful for her advice. I went back to the psychologist with my mom by my side. Ironically, the sister of one of my co-workers was a Rape Crisis Counselor. I began meeting with her as well.

      The first time I read information about Rape Trauma Syndrome, I cried. I cried hard. I was reading about myself. I thought, "Who told this person what I was going through?" It was as if they interviewed me and came into my world. Although the information was difficult to process, I continued reading. It was the first time I realized that I was not alone. It was also the first time I realized that being sexually violated was not my fault.

My Turning Point

There were days when I did not go to work. There were days when my mom would ask me if could smile, but I had nothing to smile about. On one particularly emotional day, my dad said, "This situation can make you bitter, or it can make you better. You have an opportunity to allow God to do in you what you never thought possible. Your spiritual growth can soar to greater heights during this time." When he spoke those words I did not want to hear them, but I understood exactly what he was saying. I knew deep inside that giving up was not an option, but I struggled with feeling lost in a world I thought I knew well. When I received encouragement from family and friends their words were like a cool breeze that soon faded away. I was in a trance and could not snap out of it. I was alive but not living. Breathing but not experiencing. Seeing but not connecting. I longed for my joy and my peace, but they were nowhere to be found. I wanted to approach my Heavenly Father, but I was not quite sure of what to say. I did not want the anger I felt inside to be directed toward God. I knew He loved me and I knew that He was concerned about everything that concerned me, but this was not something I was ready to discuss with Him. I knew my joy would one day be restored. I had faith that the passion for the things I loved once would be mine again. I did not know when or how, but I believed it to be so.

My Journal Entry

God knows I'll be weak. I must depend on Him. Last night was tough. My eyes filled with tears as I remembered what happened. Thoughts of this painful experience overwhelmed me to a degree. I didn't rest well and stayed home today. I've been able to go on for a while now without pondering on that day. I became sad, thinking about what am I going to do. My life has changed in its entirety. Literally, there isn't one area of my life unaffected due to this situation. As I am open and honest about my feelings, there are many days when I sit and think, not believing this has happened to me. Why has this happened to me? One would say, "Because God knows you can handle it." Well, how am I handling this? Am I handling it the right way?
Am I handling it is God's way?

One night as I sat in my living room watching television, I tuned into a program that featured women who were called to the frontline. These women were in ministry and they were talking about their painful experiences, miscarriages, broken marriages, and other difficulties they had faced. As I listened to their stories I began to weep. I could not help but to think of my current situation. I felt stained, unusable, and unlovable; like a damaged good. I definitely did not feel that I was called to the frontline. I cried out, "God, here I am…broken and humbled, I have nothing to give You. I am in need of Your love." That was the first time I cried out to God since my assault. I believe each tear was precious to Him. I did not think I had anything to give Him, but I was actually giving Him everything – my brokenness, my fears, my pain, and shattered pieces. For my own sake, I was giving Him all of me. I gave God the attention He deserved and the glory that was due to His name.

That night I exposed myself to Him. I became vulnerable. I laid everything at His feet. I worshipped Him. In tears, I asked the Lord, "In this situation, how can You be glorified?" He spoke to my heart and said, "If only all people asked that question, in all situations, at all times, concerning all things." At that moment I knew deliverance was available to me. I could finally see the light at the end of the tunnel. I still had to travel through that tunnel, but I had nothing to fear. It would be neither dark or lonely. I invited the Holy Spirit to lead and guide me every step of the way.

She Changed Me

Many days I wished I had become pregnant under different circumstances; I felt that it would have been easier to deal with. Nonetheless, I had to deal with it. I remember weighing 98 lbs. I was nauseous, dehydrated, and could not keep food or liquids down. Nurses feared my body would begin to feed on itself. Nearly each day was a mental, emotional, and or physical battle. At one point I told my family I was going to have an abortion. They responded with love, not laws or judgement. They encouraged me in ways I will forever be thankful for. They let me know that whatever decision I made they would be there for me. My dad also asked me to consider other options - give birth and maybe raise the child or allow the child to be adopted. He acknowledged that I was facing a tough decision with each choice having it's own set of pros and cons. He also wondered if I could be a source of inspiration to someone who may find themselves in a similar situation one day. After weighing all of my options, I chose not to have that abortion.

Some days I wanted to give birth and be a mother. Other days I thought it would be best to find a family to adopt the child in my womb. I met with a social worker. She explained the different types of adoption and the pros and cons that followed. I had a huge decision to make. I sat in that office feeling overwhelmed and overloaded with information. Even in that state, the social worker looked at me and said, "You're one of the ones. I know them when I see them, and you are going to be okay. You're probably going to write a book about it. You're going to be okay." Those were powerful words to a girl who at one point felt powerless.

I was very uncomfortable acknowledging the child in my womb. It was difficult because I constantly remembered the event that lead to the pregnancy, which lead to a disconnection. To touch my stomach was undesirable. I felt that if I embraced the child it meant that I would be embracing him and what he did. A friend of mine encouraged me to simply introduce myself and talk. She encouraged me to have day-to-day conversations and as if I were talking to a friend. I started by saying, "Hi, I'm Chanté!" We had simple conversations. Those simple conversations lead to prayers. Those prayers gave me the strength to love no matter what the circumstances were. This unborn child allowed me to see life in a brand new way. This child taught me that life was precious. It was worth fighting for. I did not have to do it alone because we were in it together. I kept in mind that my emotional state would significantly affect the child in my womb, so my goal was to be strong for this child. I began to fight for us both.

During my three month doctor's appointment, the gender was revealed. The child in my womb was a girl. On the screen I saw life moving inside of me. She was a busy little one! My mom said, "Baby Joy! I had a vision that it was a girl and she was full of joy. Can we call her Baby Joy?" There is a Bible verse that says, *Weeping may endure for a night, but joy comes in the morning* (Psalms 30:5 NKJV). Another verse says, *He will give you the oil of joy instead of mourning* (Isaiah 61:3). What a befitting name! We began calling her Baby Joy.

After a lot of tears, thinking, talking, listening, praying, researching, and counseling, I made the decision that Baby Joy would be adopted. It was a clear and comforting decision. I continued to love and nurture her with a love I may never truly be able to explain.

My Journal Entry #3

I have peace about blessing and releasing her to a family who will love and raise her according to God's Word. Choosing to give a child to be adopted isn't easy. You have loved and bonded with this child for nine months. I am determined to make it a joyful experience. A family will be blessed with an infant who has been nurtured in the womb. I am taking the responsibility to give birth to a child, who is not only physically healthy, but healthy in spirit as well. I pray that the perfect family for this child will be chosen. I am meeting with the adoption counselor Thursday. She will give me tips on how to deal with giving your child up for adoption. Here I go, taking closer steps toward the adoption process. This will be interesting. I thank God that I will never have to go through this again. Giving a child up for adoption is not going to be easy, so I am doing what is necessary in order to get through this in a healthy manner. I don't know anyone who's gone through this before. I'm not quite sure what I should expect. All I know is that I must continue focusing on Jesus, leaning and relying on Him every step of the way. I love this little girl.

During the early stage of my pregnancy, my mentor, who is more like a member of my family, had told me about her cousin who would be interested in adopting if I were to go that route. I texted her immediately and let her know that I would like to consider her and her husband as the adoptive parents for Baby Joy if they were still interested. Ironically, they were talking on the phone when she received my text. She confirmed that they were still interested. I met with them a few months later and we instantly developed a strong connection. I was able to get to know them and they were able to get to know me. We developed a genuine friendship. We discussed the birth plan and had it all figured out. They would come to the hospital and share in the labor experience. We would bless Baby Joy and give her to her new family. But our plan was not the Master's plan. I went into labor four weeks early. In addition to that, Baby Joy's family was on vacation celebrating their anniversary! I called to tell them that I had gone into labor and Baby Joy was in the Neonatal Intensive Care Unit (NICU). This was an emotional conversation to have. I could have told them to come immediately; in fact they wanted to, but I asked them to wait. I wanted to allow my family and those who walked with me through the pregnancy an opportunity to meet Baby Joy without feeling any discomfort on either side.

Emotions were high. Some of my family members did not want Baby Joy to be adopted, and her new family was afraid I had changed my mind. I reassured them that I had not changed my mind and allowed them access to communicate with the doctors and social worker. I wanted to give my family the time they desired with precious Baby Joy. Little did I know this time was for me as well. The hospital staff knew of my story and granted me an extended hospital stay in a special ward. I took those days to visit Baby Joy in the NICU. I also pumped milk so she would receive the best nutrients for her fragile body. When I checked out of the hospital, I continued to visit Baby

Joy daily for two weeks with pumped milk, lots of love, and heartfelt prayers. When the day came for her to be released from the NICU and given to her new parents, I chose not to be there during the transition. My dad stepped in to meet the new family at the hospital and hand Baby Joy over to her incredible parents. My decision for Baby Joy to be adopted had come to fruition. That chapter had come to a close, but it was not void of the emotional difficulty of separating from the child I carried in my womb. A few days later, once paperwork was complete, Baby Joy was heading home on an airplane with her new family.

After giving birth I was still in the process of healing from the aftermath of sexual trauma. My body was no longer the same. I experienced postpartum everything, only without the baby. My lactation nurse informed me that once Baby Joy was discharged from the hospital, it would be emotionally difficult for me to pump milk and throw it away. She explained that my body would gradually decrease the production of milk and wanted me to be prepared for the experience. Surprisingly, I was sparred. A few days after Baby Joy was discharged I took a weekend trip to the beach with my mentor and forgot my breast pump. I did not produce one drop of milk. Nor was I engorged. That was one less emotional roller coaster I would have to get on. Perhaps it was God's way of showing me some TLC-tender loving care. At that point, I stopped trying to understand everything. I knew my life was in God's hands, and that was the best place it could ever be.

I still thought about Baby Joy every day and continuously prayed for her. God gave me the strength to do something that was truly amazing. Becoming pregnant the way I did was difficult for a number of reasons. Making the decision to choose adoption was not easy, but once I took that step I knew that it was a sound decision because the reasons were so clear to me. Although my decision was made with confidence and peace, the tears still flowed.

My Journal Entry
#4

I miss her. I am sad. I wish to see her, touch her, and hold her. I'm not supposed to feel this way because I always tell myself to be strong. I felt incapable of being a mom and raising a child. I didn't think I could do it. I didn't think I would be good enough. How do I really feel? Hurt, because I can't hug her; she's gone. I didn't think it was okay to have these feelings. I thought that when you did something good, something that you knew was good without a doubt, that you wouldn't hurt. But that's not true. Sometimes you still hurt. I always feel that I am supposed to be strong. I don't allow myself to really deal with the moments. It's like a father telling his son that boys don't cry. I tell myself, you've already cried, it's time to be strong now. Sometimes I want to cry and don't, but tonight I will cry. I don't want to be fragile or broken, but memories, bittersweet memories fill my mind and I remember. I miss her.

There were days I wanted to see her, touch her, and just hear her cry. When I received pictures of her sometimes my heart would be filled with joy. Other times my heart was pained as I wondered what life would have been like had I chosen to keep her and raise her as my own. But in the end, I knew I had made the right choice and would smile on the inside with contentment.

I believe it all worked out according to His plan. God graced me in such a beautiful way! I was able to spend time with Baby Joy, release her, and bless a family desiring a child of their own. We agreed to an open adoption and our relationship continues to flourish. We are learning and growing together, and more importantly, allowing God and Baby Joy to lead the way.

PART II

The Ingredients

YOU ALONE

As I came into Your presence
I surrender all to you humbly bowed at Your throne.
For You alone, You alone can heal me.
You alone are my peace and You alone are my joy.

I'm so in love with You.
Your peace passes all understanding
Your joy gives me strength
And Your love comforts me.

As I commit my heart to You
You give me strength.
As I have faith and believe in You
You uphold me.
Lord, I surrender all to You
I sing praises to Your name
For Your love endures forever.

My Process

In the section "From My Heart to Yours", I mentioned that I gave the Lord ingredients to turn my lemons to lemonade. I could casually live my life and accept the sour lemons, or I could trust God and aggressively move forward. I could embrace the beauty that could develop from my brokenness and allow Him to take those lemons to make sweet lemonade. I chose the latter. I made a decision to give God everything. I gave Him my weaknesses, my burdens, my problems, and my fears. I also gave Him my strengths, my talents, and my accomplishments. I became transparent with God. I started by telling Him how I truly felt about myself, about my past, about the situation at hand, and about people. I wanted to experience a complete healing. Part of that healing process for me was journaling. I wrote down every issue I was dealing with- whether it was related to being sexually violated or not. I understood that many of my issues and emotional wounds began when I was sexually violated as a child. I was beginning to see how hurt I really was. I did not know how the pieces of the puzzle would come together, but I had to start somewhere. It was time to purge.

I once heard a message entitled "Trusting When Tested". This message caused my heart to sink because although I had opened my heart and allowed God to heal it, I did not want to address that deep down I was mad at Him. He was still my Heavenly Father who wrapped me in His loving arms, but I was mad at Him because I felt like He did not protect me. I did not understand how, as a child, I could be fondled and forced to perform oral copulation. I talked to God about my anger toward Him. He gently reminded me that there is evil in this world and that mankind has free will. Sometimes man takes the free will that is given and chooses to do evil things. He took me down memory lane and showed me how He has been there; how He has protected me and kept me from people and situations that would have been more detrimental to my life. He reassured me that His love is unfailing. God truly does care about everything that concerns us, and He knows when we are ready to deal with our issues. I had to be honest with myself, and honest with God. My relationship with God would not be as intimate as it is today if I had not acknowledged my anger toward Him. Exhaling the anger allowed me to inhale more of His love. This level of transparency helped me to grow in love and character.

Fighting for Emotional Freedom

When I felt comfortable sharing my story, I ordered a copy of my police report. Obtaining it was my way of saying that I was not afraid to talk about this and I was no longer ashamed. As I spoke with a sexual assault detective, I was inclined to ask a question that remained unsettled; I wanted to know how common were cases like mine where an assault took place, yet there is no conviction. The detective explained that it is very common and frustrating when they know a person committed the crime, yet they walk. She said it happens a lot to young adult women. Often the goal of the attorney prosecuting the case is to portray the victim as a liar. She further explained that it is not about what is true; it is solely about what can be proved.

For years, I was bound to the judgment of others - individuals who believed I lied and cried rape because I was pregnant. I pressed charges, yet there was no conviction. That did not look good. Hearing this detective explain how common cases like mine were, provided the validation I had been longing for.

My Journal Entry
#5

I should have never had sex with him, ever! I should have left immediately after the violation occurred. I should not have allowed him to console me and engage in intercourse following the assault. I should not have tried to fix it, I should not have kept it to myself. I should not have agreed to conduct the police report in the presence of my parents. I should have never made that call to schedule an appointment with him. I should have known better! These statements haunt me and are hindering me from healing. My self-worth is shattered, and I am embarrassed anytime I am in the presence of someone who knows about happened, but I am learning that I have to lay the negative thoughts to rest. I have to free myself, and my mind from negative thoughts. I cannot dwell on the should haves or could haves any more. I will focus on allowing God to refine me, change me, and fill me with His love.

When I encountered someone who was not sympathetic to my situation, I trained myself to leave their presence in prayer for both our sakes. I accepted the fact that I may never be able to change their perception of me, but I could change my perception of them. I made sure my perception of them remained positive and respectful.

Realizing that I could not undo the past or control the thoughts of others, I decided to focus on being made new in Christ. Before I could experience my new beginning in Christ, I had to see myself through the eyes of Christ. I memorized scriptures to rebuild my fragile spirit. I had to combat my negative thoughts with the truth of God's Word. When I focused on beautifying my spirit, my self-worth changed and so did my perspective on life. I recalled individuals in the Bible like Moses, Rahab, Joseph, and even Paul. Their beginning was not ideal. They sinned and others sinned against them, but God used them and delivered them. They submitted their lives to the Lord and He used them in a mighty way. I intentionally searched the Bible for truth concerning emotional healing, brokenness, joy, peace, love, forgiveness, and new beginnings. Here are a few Bible verses that carried me through the storm and continue to carry me now:

Come to me, all who labor and are heavy laden, and I will give you rest. Take my yoke upon you, and learn from me, for I am gentle and lowly in heart, and you will find rest for your souls.

Matthew 11:28-29 NKJV

I will instruct you and teach you in the way you should go; I will counsel you with my loving eye on you.

Psalm 32:8

Have you not known? Have you not heard? The LORD is the everlasting God, the Creator of the ends of the earth. He does not faint or grow weary; His understanding is unsearchable. He gives power to the faint, and to him who has no might He increases strength. Even youths shall faint and be weary, and young men shall fall exhausted; but they who wait for the LORD shall renew their strength; they shall mount up with wings like eagles; they shall run and not be weary; they shall walk and not faint.

Isaiah 40:28-31 ESV

Therefore, if anyone is in Christ, he is a new creation. The old has passed away; behold, the new has come.

2 Corinthians 5:17

Forget the former things; do not dwell on the past. See, I am doing a new thing! Now it springs up; do you not perceive it? I am making a way in the wilderness and streams in the wasteland.

Isaiah 43:18-19

Although I set my heart and mind to the task of being restored from the pain of my past, there were distractions. Rumors threatened to take my focus from my goal of healing. There were people praying for me along the way but there were also individuals who were not as supportive as I thought they would be. People still questioned me, looked at me funny, and believed their own version of what happened. It was difficult being around people who heard about me and treated me differently. I once even denied giving birth to Baby Joy because of the pressure of so many questions by someone who "heard" about what happened in my life. I would go so far in my healing process only to become paralyzed by the opinion of others. One day, I drew the line. I realized that I had to set some boundaries if I was going to move forward and not have my progress hindered by others. I stopped engaging with people, places, and things that were not emotionally healthy for me. At one point, my sister would check my voicemails in order to deem them as emotionally safe for me to listen to. I had to guard my healing process because I was determined to enjoy my life again.

I allowed all of my experiences to grow me in character and love. I let them revolutionize my life for the better. I positioned myself for freedom by committing myself to God's instructions. Whatever that looked like, I ran after it relentlessly and did not stop. In fact, if I wanted to experience emotional freedom, I could not abandon my healing journey. While my life was interrupted and it seemed as if someone had pressed pause, I understood that I had the power to press play and rebuild on a new foundation.

A few months after giving birth, with the support of my family and my state's Victim-Witness Compensation Program, I relocated to San Diego, CA. This was my healing place. I enrolled in a self-defense class to help regain my confidence. I joined a wonderful church and attended a women's bible study to avoid isolation. The man I married lived nearby and we grew together spiritually. This was a difficult, yet beautiful season of my life. Much healing was still needed, but I was on the right track.

Damaged or Defined?

"The man I married!" Did you catch that line in the previous paragraph? Do you remember when I said I thought I was a damaged good? I never thought I would get married. I never thought I would have that type of love. From my view, there was nothing left to be desired. I did not think I had what a man required, but God gave me beauty for ashes, and my husband saw in me what I could not see.

I met my husband Howard when I was 21. We had a long distance relationship for a few years, and then I broke up with him. I told him I needed to get my life in order. Fortunately, our friendship remained intact. One Easter Sunday, he texted me a message that said, "Happy Resurrection Sunday". I did not intend on responding, but I knew it was not right to ignore him. A few weeks later, I gave him a call. When he asked how I was doing, I told him all that had transpired. Surely, that was the last thing he imagined he would hear. But from that moment on, he stood by my side and showed the utmost support. He emailed me daily with a scripture and words of encouragement. He once prayed over the child in my womb, and when I went into preterm labor, he was there. During my extended stay at the hospital, he was there. When I was an emotional mess, he was there. Then the day came. He proposed and I said, "Yes!" But with that "yes" came mixed emotions. I was both elated and afraid at the same time. I cared for him and I did not want to ruin his life with my issues. Gratefully, he assured me that we would do life together, and that he would continue to stand with me. Someone asked him what was special about me that made him choose me as his wife. He responded, "She is the first woman I have dated who put God before me." What a high compliment! I knew without a doubt, I was safe in his arms.

Our wedding was a beautiful and joyous affair! Baby Joy and her parents were there. Her mom was my make-up artist and our soloist. I could not have asked for anything more. But when the day was over, I quickly learned that in the midst of all the beauty and bliss of marriage, triggers from rape are real. I was triggered on my wedding night and many nights after that. Some triggers caused me to experience sadness, because I still had the memories of being raped. While others triggers were followed by fear and anger. Though my husband was supportive, my triggers affected him. Triggers became the elephant in the room. We knew they were there, but we did not talk about them. We did not know how to talk about them. Intimacy with my husband was difficult. I was not even sure of how to deal with that reality. I would sometimes call my mom, who was also sexually violated, crying, asking her when the triggers would end. She would give me advice and would always suggest I pray and talk to my husband. I also talked to a staff member at the rape crisis center and more importantly, I talked to my husband. He would remind me that I was safe and he was extremely patient with me. We prayed and we created a plan on how to overcome those triggers. With the help of the Holy Spirit and an open line of communication with one another, we overcame!

All of my triggers were not sexually related. While on a business trip, a company I worked for paid for a massage at the resort's day spa. On that monumental day, I took back all control. I was nervous, and as the memories began to resurface,

I told myself that it was time I take back what was taken from me - a relaxing massage. I requested a female masseuse, and I talked to her the entire time. I cannot tell you how awesome it felt to experience this level of empowerment. Another time I recall when I saw the name of the man who raped me on a product description of an item I purchased. I threw the item across the room and sat on my bedroom floor crying. I was mad at myself for crying over it. My husband came in the room and sat by my side. When I told him what was going on, he held me saying, "That name has no power over you." I thought about the song that says that there is power in the name of Jesus, and the Bible verse in James 2:19 that speaks of demons trembling at the name of Jesus. I made up my mind that I was not going to allow the name of the man who raped me to have power over me! I still have that product in my home. The rapist did not get the victory!

I have learned that healing is a process. When triggers come I no longer fall apart; I have a plan. Most of the time I write in my journal to process what I am feeling in order to identify and understand the trigger. I do not suppress my emotions. If I want to cry, I cry. If I want to scream, I scream. As long as it is emotionally and physically healthy, I do want I need to do to ground myself. I talk to my husband and I also talk to God. I know that if He brought me this far, He will not leave me on my own to figure out how to overcome these triggers.

Forgiveness, Love, and Mercy

Forgiveness and love were key factors in my healing process. In the beginning, I did not want to discuss forgiveness, and definitely not love. Layers of unhealthy emotions had to be stripped away before I would be able to confidently say that I was free indeed, and when I applied Matthew 6:14-15 to my healing process, my freedom was complete. It reads, *For if you forgive other people when they sin against you, your heavenly Father will also forgive you. But if you do not forgive others their sins, your Father will not forgive your sins.* I forgave by sending away the hurt that was on my heart, and after being set free, I had a heart of mercy and love.

LAYER #1:

There were days full of anger, feeling frustrated in my healing process, and hateful toward the man who raped me. One day in particular, I was ready to tell him how I truly felt, I looked in the mirror and cried. I began talking and writing what I held inside for so long:

"I want it back, everything you took from me. I want it back. I want my self-respect, I want my confidence, I want my joy, peace, my love. I want it all back. I am angry. I am badly wounded and deeply hurt. Do you know this? I cry often. Has there been justice? Do you cry? How do you feel? How do you think Baby Joy will feel? I have to tell her something. What do I tell her? I live, but I do not live free, not whole, but broken; a piece of me is gone. How does this all work? I feel the chains holding me down, the walls keeping me in, and the pain keeping me silent. Afraid to love, afraid to live, afraid to dream. No longer social, no longer free. You trapped me. I am angry at this pain. I want it to go away. I am angry at the thoughts. I want them to disappear. Go! Go far from me never to return. Let me be free! Let me live again! Let me dream! I want to love. You said that you didn't know what came over you. I bet you also didn't know how you ruined me; you stained me. You turned all of my light into darkness. You killed me! You killed the inside of me. You're a killer, a murderer, a thief. You stole from me and I want it back. Don't speak to me. Don't touch me. Just give it all back to me! Just give it back to me! It is not yours. It does not belong to you. I didn't give it to you-- no not that time. You stink. You're ugly. Everything about you is ugly! Now I need help. I need to be healed. I need to be set free. Set free from you-- set free from everything and everyone. Every scar, every hurt, every excuse, every reason-- everything. You caused this, you should fix it. Now do it. Just do it. I really don't like you. I hate you; but I can't. I have to love you, and I have to forgive you. Why? Because that's where my healing begins. Okay, well, I need help getting there. Better yet, I don't need you to do it. I don't need or want your help at all. With God's help, I will do it. I release the pain and I will fill my heart with love. I will show mercy. The same mercy that God would show me. Now let the healing begin.....please. **I AM TIRED OF HURTING! IT'S WEARING ME DOWN AND OUT**. I can't go on like this. I gave birth to a child because life is precious. I have to live my life like it is precious too. It's hard, that's the truth. It's hard. You don't make it any easier, but in the aftermath, I will be stronger!"

Releasing my feelings was my way of going off on him-- of telling him how I felt in case he did not know. While venting, which I strongly believe was healthy, I realized that I could not stay in that place. As you read, I chose to forgive. This was the first step to release him and his influence on my life. Forgiveness was a major turning point in my healing process. Releasing the offense positioned me to receive the healing.

LAYER #2:
I had been praying more often. I also had been reading what the Bible says about love, walking in love, and being confident in Christ. One night while studying the Bible, I felt that I needed to go in the other room and pray as my husband slept. As I began praying, the names of people I knew were coming to my mind, and I would pray for them. I prayed for their health, their purpose, and protection. Then the name of the guy who assaulted me came to my mind and I felt reluctant. Initially I struggled, but because I sent the offense away, I was in a position to show mercy. I prayed for him as earnestly as I had for everyone else. Afterwards, there was a beautiful release. Glory to God!

LAYER #3:

One day while at home, I yelled, "I want to be free!" I had made a lot of progress, but something was lingering and I could not figure it out. I had grown in character and confidence. Still, I was longing for an "it is finished" experience.

Later that day, the Lord responded to my heart's cry. He instructed me to write letters to the individuals who sexually violated me. I looked up and said, "Really, Lord?" I wondered what would be the purpose of these letters. I had already forgiven and sent away the offenses. I was not hurt nor was I ashamed. So why write these letters? Then, the Lord made it clear, this was the continuation of showing mercy. Not that I had to deliver the letters to them, but I needed to write them.

In those letters, which took a few days to write, I prayed that those who violated me would experience God's grace and understand His love for them. I blessed them and prayed that they would be delivered from all things that keep them bound. I prayed that they would repent for any sin they had in their lives so that their prayers and blessings would not be blocked. I prayed for their lineage. I became sympathetic towards them. I called them out of darkness into the marvelous light. I told them I loved them and I prayed that they too would be free indeed.

I wrote with a renewed understanding of what God's assignment for me was. Doing so gave me a peace and a freedom that I did not anticipate. That day, I learned that loving earnestly runs deep. It is everlasting, and it never fails. It is about making a decision to love no matter what- even when it is not popular and when it is uncomfortable. I learned to love with the same kind of love that Christ loves me with. In other words, I've learned to have a mindset towards those who violated me that says, "You're not right, and I know it. But, I am still going to love you." There will be heartaches, pain, and deep disappointments to come, but I now know that I can walk in love and forgiveness toward others, because that is what Christ does with me.

Below, you will find the very letters that confused me initially, but opened my eyes to what it means to love earnestly and show mercy, by God's grace:

1st LETTER

I remember the night my dad picked me up from class and told me that you had been killed. I cried so hard! It was hard to hear this horrible news. I also remember wondering why I cared. I could not understand why I cried when I heard that you had been murdered. You, the person who in my childhood, made me perform oral sex. Nonetheless, it is many years later, and I am writing this letter to you. You were the first person to violate me sexually. I never understood why you would tell me to perform oral sex and then tell me that if I said anything, I would get in trouble. You would also give me candy or money to buy candy. I remember this happening a few times. I forgive you. I do not know what led you to do it. I hate that something or someone influenced you to be that way. You are no longer here on earth, and I have no idea where you will spend eternity. What I do know is that I love you. There is no way I love what you did, but I love the person God created, and I release you and all the negative influence that has hindered me from being free indeed. I am turning away and ending this letter now. I end in love. Not in my own strength. It is purely by God's grace.

Sincerely,
Chanté

2nd LETTER

I remember what happened to me over 15 years ago as if it were yesterday. I never recalled any unpleasant moments with you until that day. Everyone was having a good time. I broke something; I do not remember all of the details, except that you said not to worry. You said you would take care of it and fix it, and you touched me as you said that. The fondling did not last long, yet it was beyond inappropriate, and you told me to "shhh", and I did. I "shhh'd" and I was in shock. I HATE that that happened. I hate that I did not stand up to you and tell! Now, I am writing this letter because this is my time to love on you, and release you. Not only release you, but all that has hindered me from being free indeed. I start by saying, "I love you". I love that you are made in the image of God. I do not know where you are regarding your relationship with the Lord and your level of transparency with Him. I pray that you are free. Free indeed. Free from your past and delivered from the chains of the enemy. I pray that your children are blessed, and you are the godly father God has called you to be. May the peace of God and the joy of the Lord fill your days. As I speak your name I smile, and I say I love you. My heart rejoices that you are continually drawing near to the Lord and experiencing His great love for you. May the joy of the Lord be your strength in all that you do.

Sincerely,
Chanté

3rd LETTER

This letter is a letter of love to you. I am learning that love is not just the romance we see on television or the passion we hear in a song. It is a God-given source of healing and wholeness. My love for you is not sensual; it is a spirit-filled, God-given love. I have written to you in my journal before, first words of hate, and anger. Finally, words of forgiveness. I have also prayed for you. This letter is somewhat different. I am writing to release love. Clearly, I do not hold the world in my hands, but I know the One who does. He has instructed me, by His Holy Spirit, great sovereignty, and empowerment, to love on you like never before. Carnally, this is absurd and borderline sickening, but I am quickly reminded that I am not to be carnally minded, and that this battle I fight is spiritual, not carnal. I do pray that you are well; more than that, I pray that you have a personal relationship with Jesus Christ. I pray this so that you can experience freedom and live the abundant life in Christ. You are fearfully and wonderfully made, and I thank the Lord that you will always know your value and remain confident in Christ. You were known by God before you were in your mother's womb, and He, your Creator, already knew the plans He had for you. I pray that you come to know your purpose and run with it if you have not already done so. May the protection of God and the favor of the Lord be upon you. Rest in His peace and never doubt His great love for you.

Sincerely,
Chanté

My Journal Entry #6

God forgives me when I sin. Therefore, when others sin against me, I open my heart to God; I share my concerns with Him. I pray for those who have sinned against me. I extend forgiveness and I release the offense. When I am broken, I will cast my cares upon Him because He cares for me (Psalm 55:22, 1 Peter 5:7). I lay my burdens at His feet. I will find comfort in knowing that He cares for me and I will rest in His perfect peace (Isaiah 26:3). When I need direction I ask the Lord for wisdom (James 1:5). I rest in knowing that He orders my steps (Psalm 119:33). When I am afraid, I am reminded that the Word tells me to fear not because God is with me always (Isaiah 41:10). I am reminded that my God will never leave me nor forsake me (Deuteronomy 31:8). When I am weak, He is strong (2 Corinthians 12:9).

The Lemonade

HEAL. LOVE. LIVE.

Hurting others revealed I was still hurting.
Wanting to see them suffer revealed I was still suffering.
Not wanting them to succeed revealed I was
not succeeding.

Forgiving revealed I no longer wanted to
be controlled by my painful past.
Loving revealed I had finally understood God's
unconditional love for me.

Praying for them to be set free revealed I understood
God's mercy toward me. And now, I am healed,
loving earnestly, and living life free!

My Purpose

Two years after being raped, I heard these words in my heart, "It's time". A few days later, on a Sunday evening, I was online and conducted a search for Bay Area rape crisis centers. I did not plan on looking this up, but when the thought came to me I began typing. The first search result was an informational page on rape published by Bay Area Women Against Rape. I was drawn to the section titled "How to Help". I acted on it. I called their office that Monday morning and filled out an application to join their next rape crisis counselor training session.

I was nauseous and nervous the first night of training. I questioned myself. I did not know if I was ready to help others heal from something I was still dealing with. I was also alarmed when I saw that the trainer was a male. All of those fears were quieted when he said, "Hi, my name is Howard." He had the same name as my husband! I felt like I belonged there.

My training took an unexpected turn the night we learned about adults who were sexually violated as children. As we viewed a documentary and discussed the effects, I tried to fight the tears, but I could not. It was all too real for me. As I opened up about being sexual violated as a child, I received the support of our trainers, who patiently allowed me to process that moment. During a different night of training, one of the instructors said, "A man or woman who is raped will do what they have to do to survive mentally, emotionally, and physically. People will ask the survivor why they did or did not do 'A, B, or C'? The answer is, 'It was that or go insane; that or go crazy.' Survivors will do what they feel is necessary in order to regain power." This was the answer to my own why. I did not take pleasure in being raped. Having intercourse afterwards was my way of renaming the assault and regaining control. It breaks my heart to know that there are individuals suffering in silence because they do not know how to process sexual trauma and they question their response to being violated.

Becoming a rape crisis counselor empowered me in ways I didn't think were possible. I advocated for the survivors. I talked to them on the hotline as well as face-to-face during in-person counseling sessions. I sat with them in the hospital and at the police station. I remembered what it was like to need someone by your side. As I empowered them, I too became empowered. It was a beautiful exchange. It was also the beginning of an understanding that my pain serves a higher purpose than me.

Once, I was at a women's Bible study for moms, and one of the leaders asked us to pray for a young girl who had been raped and became pregnant. She had an abortion. She was having a hard time processing the rape, and she was also concerned about her safety because the man who raped her was to be released soon. Before my brain could catch up with what was in my heart, I said, "I'll pray for her. I was raped. I also became pregnant, and I can talk to her if she wants to talk." Once my brain caught up, I sat there asking myself, "What in the world did you say that for? No one asked you to say all of that." I will never forget that moment. That's when I knew it was in me. I did not plan on saying anything nor did I sign up to speak those words ahead of time. When I heard of the familiar pain, my spirit jolted. The leader later connected that young girl and her mother with me. We met in person on a weekly basis, then transitioned to weekly phone calls. Helping her felt natural and purposeful.

My heart's desire is that everyone who has endured any form of sexual trauma would experience emotional healing. I have developed a level of transparency with my story, which I never thought I would have. It took time for my transparency to be at the level it is at now. I owe it all to my God. He continues to give me the grace to share and help others cross over to the other side, from hurt to healed. In 2015 I sat in my bedroom, praying and journaling. During that time, God put it on my heart to start an organization that would help women who had experienced sexual violation heal.

I remember feeling like it was too big of a challenge, but I could not ignore it. I began writing what I saw, regarding how to help them heal. Afterwards I thought, "Lord, You have given this to me, but what do I call it?" Over the next few days I brainstormed and bounced names to my husband and family, but nothing stuck. I went to my bedroom and closed the door. I said, "Lord, and I am not leaving this room until I have a name for what You put in my heart to do. You told me what to do; surely You have a name for it." The name Earnest Love, Inc. was birthed that day, and my husband added "Heal, Love, Live" as the slogan. God explained that there is a love that can heal all hurts and emotional wounds. This love is His love, and it is earnest. It is sincere, heartfelt, intense, and unconditional. When we receive His love, we heal; we love ourselves and others. We then begin living a beautiful and abundant life.

As I reflect on all of my experiences, I see how my life could have become sour. I could have marinated in the pain and anger. But I chose to move forward. I stopped asking, "Why me?" Instead, I began saying, "Lord, I am available to You. What would you have me to do?" I gave God my sour lemons and in return, He gave me the sweet lemonade! He has done more in me than I ever thought possible. He has given me beauty for ashes. I am a witness that there is purpose in your pain. I have found that God has a skillful way of creating masterpieces out of shattered pieces. Will you trust Him to do something magnificent in your life too?

What Matters Most

We all have a story and one day, our stories will end. I pray that yours will end in victory. The way to guarantee that it does is by accepting Jesus Christ as your Lord and Savior. He died on the cross for our sins and rose again, so that we could live abundantly. Accepting Jesus Christ as Lord of all is the most important decision you will ever make. If you have never prayed the prayer of salvation, let today be the day. If you need to rededicate your life to Christ, let today be the day. John 3:16 says, *For God so loved the world, that He gave His only Son, that whoever believes in Him should not perish but have eternal life.* If you are ready to proclaim that eternal life, pray this prayer with me:

*Father God, I confess that I am a sinner
and I ask you to forgive me of my sins.
Thank you for loving me unconditionally
and sending your son to die for me.
I believe that Jesus Christ died on the cross
for my sins and rose again so I can be free.
Today, I choose to follow Him.
I accept Jesus Christ into my heart
as my Lord and Savior. Amen!*

Welcome to the family! Do you know that there is a celebration in Heaven right now? There sure is because your name has been added to the Lamb's Book of Life! Praise the Lord, I am rejoicing too! We serve a loving God who created us in His image, and His love for you will never run dry.

I pray this message of restoration will be embedded in your heart. I pray that you will overcome all unhealthy attachments to your past. I pray that your past will no longer hinder you, but propel you into your purpose so that you can excel in what God has called you to do.

Joy

What is it that keeps me going in the midst
of trials and storms?

When I have no solutions to the problems at hand

And seem to be lost in this troublesome land?

My mind can't do enough to keep me in this state,

It's the joy of the Lord that makes me feel this way.

No matter what comes my way, no matter
what seems to be at stake.

The joy of the Lord fills my heart and I will not break.

I can't stop thinking about what He's done for me.

He's brought me through so much, oh how
merciful is He.

The joy of the Lord is my strength and I rely upon
it each day.

I continue to see my God make a way
out of no way.

Your Turn

You may be wondering, "Where do I go from here? I have read your story, I have given my heart to Christ, or I have rededicated my life, now what?" Well, the last chapter of this book is your chapter. There are treasures inside of you waiting to be uncovered, and it is not too late for the great reveal! It is time to heal from your painful past and let love do it's work so that you can live life to its fullest. Start working on your lemonade recipe today. Begin to process your painful experience(s) by giving God all of your ingredients and allow Him to add His own. Our recipes will look different because our ingredients are not the same. We have many differences, but each of us needs God's ingredients to complete our recipe. I am confident that you will experience a higher level of greatness as you heal emotionally and grow spiritually. When you cross over to the other side from hurt to healed and you are pursuing a life of joy and happiness, indulge yourself in your sweet and refreshing lemonade. But do more than that; consider sharing a glass with someone else. I believe that sharing is a crucial part of the healing process.

Your Lemonade Recipe

What about you? What is your story? What sour experience(s) do you need to deal with? Rather sexual or non-sexual, no situation is too big or too small to acknowledge. If you have not healed from it, it is worth mentioning.

_____

_____

_____

_____

_____

_____

_____

_____

_____

_____

_____

_____

_____

_____

_____

_____

Many people, who do not give God a chance, miss out on the beauty of life. The first downfall they experience, they give up, deny, and reject God. They forget and fail to believe that He wants to restore them. God will not make you serve Him, but He truly desires that you will. God is concerned about everything you go through. What do you want to say to God? What cares and burdens do you need to give Him? What is He speaking to your heart?

_____

_____

_____

_____

_____

_____

_____

_____

_____

_____

_____

_____

_____

_____

_____

_____

After experiencing trauma, the memories remain. People, places, and things can trigger you from time to time. When triggered, I believe it is important to have a plan for how to work through these unsettling and overwhelming moments. This plan is your Toolbox. I have one, and encourage you to create one of your own. Below is an example of a Toolbox:

Sample Toolbox:

- Pray (talk to God about it)
- Call your counselor or mentor
- Journal what you are feeling
- Workout
- Take a walk
- Sing
- Listen to music
- Cry
- Dance
- Read your favorite Bible verses
- Read inspirational quotes
- Listen to a motivational message
- Reflect on how far you have come
- Speak positive affirmations
- Hold or look at something that represents peace or freedom

What is in your Toolbox? You can start by listing who or what empowers you. You can also write healthy ways to release stress. It may also help to consider when and where you feel most peaceful and relaxed.

Wounded emotions produce wounded relationships and can even affect friendships. Has the pain of your past affected your relationships? What do you and your friends, family members, significant other, or spouse need to discuss in order to foster a more healthy relationship?

_____

_____

_____

_____

_____

_____

_____

_____

_____

_____

_____

_____

_____

_____

_____

_____

What distractions are deterring you from experiencing freedom? What changes can you make in order to remain spiritually, emotionally, and physically healthy? What type of boundaries do you need to create in order to protect your healing process?

_____

_____

_____

_____

_____

_____

_____

_____

_____

_____

_____

_____

_____

_____

_____

_____

_____

Look up Bible verses that pertain to your situation. Write them down. Meditate on them and allow the Word of God to breathe new life into your spirit. (Example: 2 Corinthians 5:17 *Therefore, if anyone is in Christ, the new creation has come. The old has gone, the new is here!*)

Transparency is necessary if you want to experience emotional freedom. When our wounded emotions are not dealt with, the result is like an infection, contaminating other areas in our lives. Acknowledge the wounded emotions that continue to haunt you and explain why.

I heard a pastor say, "You can't be angry with people and say they weren't there for you when you needed them." He explained that some people are not equipped to handle your situation. Your situation may have triggered them. They themselves may be dealing with their own issues of guilt, shame, and pain. If someone is not equipped to handle your situation, do not hold that against them. Take this time to acknowledge how the opinions of others have affected you. Who said hurtful words to you? What offenses do you need to release?

_____

_____

_____

_____

_____

_____

_____

_____

_____

_____

_____

_____

_____

_____

_____

Sometimes we justify why harm is done to us, and even blame ourselves for the damage that is done to us by others. I urge you not to take responsibility for the actions of others. That is a burden you should not carry. This is a good time to write statements that reverse the negative words and thoughts you have been telling yourself regarding blame and shame, or any unhealthy beliefs. For example you may write, "I will not feel guilty because of someone else's actions. I did not make him/her violate me. I will no longer see myself as a victim. I am victorious and I am loved by God."

Are the offenses of others hindering you from moving forward in freedom? Take this time to release the hurts and offenses and receive God's love for you and rest in His peace.

How can your pain propel you into purpose? Have you asked God how He can be glorified? You may not have all the answers to these questions today, but God does. As I stated earlier, He has a skillful way of creating masterpieces out of shattered pieces. Pray and ask God for strategy on how to move forward.

_____

_____

_____

_____

_____

_____

_____

_____

_____

_____

_____

_____

_____

_____

_____

_____

_____

_____

_____

By now, you have realized that life consists of mountain high and valley low experiences. I have learned in the midst of it all, I can stay grounded if I guard my heart and stay rooted in biblical principles. When I feel unsettled or overwhelmed, I refer to what I call "golden nuggets" to keep me on track. With God, I can protect my peace and my joy. When I am offended, I can choose to release the offense in order to maintain my freedom!

My Golden Nuggets:

- Release the offense
- Receive God's love
- Extend love and forgiveness
- Pray for those who hurt me
- Always ask God for direction and wisdom
- Live to please God, not man
- Rest if I must, but don't give up
- Inspire others
- Talk to someone
- Remind myself that in Christ I am strong enough to conquer even this
- Release it, because holding on allows very little room for future greatness